Blue Smoke.

A Book of Verses by
Karle Wilson Baker.

The flame of my life burns low
Under the cluttered days,
Like a fire of leaves.
But always a little blue, sweet-smelling smoke
Goes up to God.

New Haven:
Yale University Press.
London : Humphrey Milford : Oxford University Press.
Mdccccxix.

Contents.

Foreword.

THE poems included in this book have been written at intervals since 1901. It is inevitable, therefore, that some of them should embody outgrown moods, and that there should be something here and there, in the way of gesture or costume, that I no longer find natural or characteristic. But to claim exemption from irrelevant tests is only to appeal to those severer ones which are permanently valid; and that appeal I must make, with what assurance I may.

I am indebted to the following periodicals for permission to reprint poems which first appeared in their pages: *The Yale Review, Harper's, Scribner's,* the *Century,* the *Atlantic Monthly, Poetry* (Chicago), the *Sonnet,* the *Smart Set,* the *Little Review,* the *Colonnade,* the *Poetry Review of America,* the *Texas Review, McClure's,* the *Outlook,* the *Cosmopolitan, Everybody's,* the *Writer's Magazine, Munsey's,* the *Delineator,* the *Woman's Magazine,* the *Southern Woman's Magazine,* and *Lippincott's.*

KARLE WILSON BAKER.

Daily Bread.

MY little town is homely as another,
But it is old,
And it is full of trees,
And it is covered with sky.
My heart lives in a little house with a fire in it,
And a pillow at night,
And is fed daily by laughter and cares,
And the dear needs of children;
But my soul lives out of doors.
Its bread is the beauty of trees,
Its drink, the sky.
There is a moment on winter evenings
When the grey trees on the near hills turn rosy,
And all the smoke is blue.
Then I go forth with my basket for manna.
And sometimes,
When the air is very clear,
And the moon comes before the dark,
God himself brings me green wine in a cup of silver,
And holds it for me
While I drink.

Altair.

THREE of them walk together
  Joyous and fair and high,
Through the still, heavenly weather
Up in the summer sky. . . .

Under their feet are the fountains
The night-bird's heart outpours
Flooding the mimic mountains
Of the shadowy sycamores.

Over the sky forever
She leadeth her comrades sweet;
No dream of our mortal fever
Troubleth her straying feet.

She lifteth the years from my shoulders,
She looseth the weight from my wings;
Long hidden from all beholders
An old, sealed fountain sings. . . .

Three of them walk together—
She is the fairest of three;
And sweet as the heavenly weather
She maketh the heart of me!

Days.

SOME days my thoughts are just cocoons—all cold, and dull, and blind,
They hang from dripping branches in the grey woods of my mind;

And other days they drift and shine—such free and flying things!
I find the gold-dust in my hair, left by their brushing wings.

A Clear Night.

I HAVE worn this day as a fretting, ill-made garment,
Impatient to be rid of it.

And lo, as I drew it off over my shoulders
This jewel caught in my hair.

The Rain-pool.

MY life is like a little pool
Left by the passing rain
Beside the village thoroughfare
Where every path is plain;

A brown and useful little pool
For childhood's dimpled glee,
And thirsty dogs, and paddling ducks
Who stir it mightily!

(But oh, it is so still and blue, beside the evening street,
When little, wary stars come down, to cool their twinkling
feet!)

Winter Secrets.

GOD wrote my heart a letter, I believe,
And used the branches of the naked trees
Against the winter sky, for characters.
I cannot translate into mortal words
The dainty hieroglyphics of the elm,
The oracles in oak, the willow's rhyme,
Nor any of the lovely dialects
That write themselves across the setting sun.
But, like some tonsured pedant of old time
Who wooed his dimming parchment like a bride,
And pored upon it, yearning, day and night,
So, year by year, I take my lesson up,
And dream out little meanings, one by one,
Writ in the margin of God's manuscript.

Of Italy.

WHEN I was young, it seemed to me
That I should die for Italy!
The beauty of my native glade
Was as a barefoot beggar-maid
To some proud youth, who burned the while
And fainted for a princess' smile.

Now I am older, and I see
Such beauty in a poplar-tree,
Such pathos in my village spire
Against the sudden western fire—
Passion to make the spirit swoon
In black boughs etched upon the moon—
Till now it sometimes seems to me
That I should die of Italy!

Thrushes.

THROUGH Tanglewood the thrushes trip,
As brown as any clod,
But in their spotted throats are hung
The vesper-bells of God.

And I know little secret truths,
And hidden things of good,
Since I have heard the thrushes sing
At dusk, in Tanglewood.

Good Company.

TODAY I have grown taller from walking with the trees,
The seven sister-poplars who go softly in a line;
And I think my heart is whiter for its parley with a star
That trembled out at nightfall and hung above the pine.

The call-note of a redbird from the cedars in the dusk
Woke his happy mate within me to an answer free and fine;
And a sudden angel beckoned from a column of blue smoke—
Lord, who am I that they should stoop—these holy folk of thine?

The Poet.

SAY'ST thou the heart hath missed her harvestings—
A muffled harp, no hand to stir the rust?
Some note shall yet be struck from out the strings
That shall go singing when thy heart is dust.

Then soft, tread softly, clamorous heart bereft,
The lamentable chamber of thy years!
Fame brews her nectar from the sweet drops left
In broken jars where Love hath stored his tears.

The Lost One.

THERE are so many kinds of me
Indeed, I cannot say
Just which of many I shall be
Tomorrow, or today.

Whence are they—princess, witch or nun?
I know not; this I know:
The gravest, gentlest, simplest one
Was buried long ago.

Wrapped in the faded pride it wore,
It slumbers, as is fit,
And nothing tells the name it bore
Or marks the place of it.

But all the other kinds of me,
They know, and turn aside,
And check their laughter soberly
Above the one that died.

The Return.

AND so at last I trod the ways
I once had found so fair,
To find the rose of memory
Had drooped and faded there.

Noon on the strange-familiar ways;
Dust, and the common things;
Until at last the day spread out
For flight its lovely wings,

And let their golden shadows fall
Across the fields I knew;
And then the sudden splendor came
As it was wont to do.

Like the old smile across a face
Whose early charm is spent,
That light of unforgotten days
Trembled—and came—and went!

The Lost Ideal.

'TIS not because I loved you in those years,
Those early years that will not come again;
That would not wake this wan old ghost of pain
Who walks a stranger to the balm of tears;

Not that my spirit worshipped at your feet
And made no marvel of so plain a thing;
I would not grudge the bluebird to the spring,
Nor wish an April niggard of her sweet;

Not what I gave, but something that I missed,
Vexes my vision of the vanished years:
Not that young love stored up so many tears,
But that you broke the vase of amethyst!

Lights.

THEY are lighting the lamps in the fishing-port, where the dories anchored lie,
And over the steeple a little moon hangs thin and sweet in the sky.
The calm lights come as I pace the sand and I would they were calm for me;
But the cry of the past comes out of the vast like a signal-light at sea.

The blue smoke curls from the fisher's hut; faint comes the children's shout.
Over the breast of the rosy bay the yellow lamps stream out.
Oh, the lamps are lit by the fishers' wives, and sweet with content they be;
But a light burns dim on the sea's far rim that was lamp and star to me.

Oh, all is safe in the fishing-port, and kind are the fisher-folk,
And sweet is the light of the sturdy lamps and friendly the curling smoke.
Ay, hearty and kind are the fisher-folk—but how should they know of me
How my thoughts beat back o'er the buried track of a ship long lost at sea?

Love's Return.

THE thorn beside the garden gate had stood all winter bare;
Today, behold, the sudden green was all a-twitter there!

Today I visited my heart—I'd left it stark and lorn—
And little throstle-throated joys were singing in the thorn!

The Spendthrifts.

FOR jewels in the mines of Pain
He delved with labor long:
One only crumbled not to dust—
One little opal song.

He poured the red wine of his heart
To bathe unworthy feet;
The world's rejected came from far
To drain the chalice sweet.

He plunged his hot and reckless youth
Death-deep in battle-dins;
They wove a garment of his scars
And covered up his sins.

So—Poet, Lover, Patriot, all—
They fling their wealth away:
The common wisdom of the wise
Is not for such as they;

The prudent treasures of the wise
The dust shall level o'er;
God's simple ones may trust to Fame
To guard their slender store!

The Difference.

WHEN I was a little child
The Day, a princess bright,
Was always running, to escape
The ogre of the Night.

But now I am a woman grown,
Day clambers up the steep,
Where Night, the Mother, waits to still
Her sobbing babe to sleep.

Gossamer.

OUT of the common sun and stress
I weave a cunning happiness:
A cobweb, fine and frail and fair,
That trembles in the passing air.

God lets me work till it is done,
A breath of silver in the sun:
He does not mind—unless I cry
When His great, wrecking winds go by.

Bethesda.

WITHIN the mystic porches five
My Dreams lie sick and spent;
Waiting, weary, scarce alive,
Withered, impotent.

The pool is still as if it sleeps,
By not a whisper fanned;
Motionless in the heavy deeps
The mirrored pillars stand.

There, silently, from morn to noon,
Those hapless cripples sit:
God send, the absent Angel soon
May come and trouble it!

O Knowest Thou.

O KNOWEST thou the wings of Love, belovèd?
Hast seen their light beyond the harbor-bar?
A tenderness at dawn above the meadows,
A shimmering athwart the evening star?
Methinks they pass in song of distant waters;
They hover in the whisper of the grove;
O fairest of the spinning planet's daughters,
Say, knowest thou the shining wings of Love?

O knowest thou the feet of Love, belovèd?
Hast heard his silent feet amid the press?
Or seekest thou among the pathless places
And solitary stretches waterless?
The lowliest of the caravan that passes
Along the way where all the weary move
Can point thee, Sweet, among the common grasses,
The footprints of the patient feet of Love!

The Tree.

MY life is a tree,
Yoke-fellow of the earth;
Pledged,
By roots too deep for remembrance,
To stand hard against the storm,
To fill my Place.
(But high in the branches of my green tree there is a wild
bird singing:
Wind-free are the wings of my bird: she hath built no
mortal nest.)

The Love of Elia.

"Methinks it is better that I should have pined away seven of my goldenest years, when I was thrall to the fair hair and fairer eyes of Alice W——n, than that so passionate a love-adventure should be lost."

HER image glides from page to page,
A Presence, frail and fair,
Scarce more than sweet averted face
And glint of shining hair;
Yet if she went a light would fade
And leave a shadow there.

His Alice! From the well-worn page
That in the firelight lies
Before me, child, I see with him
Out of the embers rise
That unforgotten face of thine—
Fair hair, and fairer eyes.

Perhaps thy gentle arms grew old
From Love's sweet burdens free.
Listen! These prattling little ones
Love brought to him and thee—
These dear Dream-Children with deep eyes
That nestle at his knee!

Nay, what if darker Fate drew near,
Forbade unvexed to pine,
And bowed thy comely head to take
The heavy crown divine

From hands less reverent than those
Of that old love of thine,

Bowed thy cold lips in bitterness
To desecrated streams:
Still bright along his quiet ways
Thy virgin vesture gleams;
To him thou still art spirit-wife,
Maid-mother of his dreams.

So for the tale of later years,
Sweet child, we scarcely care:
Sure, 'twere enough beatitude
For mortal maid to wear,—
Thy mystical maternity,
Sweet Alice with fair hair,

Thou gentlest love of searing Fame!
Frail, favored child of Fate!
He hoards thy memory chaste and sweet
While newer faces wait;
And the dear ashes of his love
He keeps inviolate.

The Fleets of My Fancy.

THE fleets of my fancy
  Stir but to the winds of Fate;
They skim like gulls when the winds blow—
In the calm, they wait.

The tides of my spirit
Obey but the moon of Fate;
The Great Deep cometh and goeth
Secret, elate.

The Winds of God.

(1906)

THE wind is blowing across the world; it is lifting my brother's hair
Freshly from off his forehead, and bringing the light to his eyes;
Listen, and you may hear it come, stirring the empty air:
Oh, lift your faces, folk of the world, and feel the wind arise!

Feel it? Ay, you may see it far, in the tops of the gusty trees
Where the beam of a day that is passing borrows a poignant grace;
And some are scattered before the gale, like a leaf that flutters and flees—
But we that have waited long stand up and take it full in the face!

It comes, and we know not whither; it hastens we know not where;
And boisterous is its coming, the swoop of its healing wings;
Yet dainty as breath of clover-fields it washes in waves of air
O'er a wistful world that had half forgot to dream of its visitings.

No blame to our patient fathers, they born to the moment of calm;
The great winds blow not alway; the storm itself must rest;

They shunned not the wounds of the weary fight, though
their wise men knew no balm:
Though the air was stale and empty, they breathed it and
did their best.

But ours was the happy cradle, the trough of the rising
wave;
Up to its crested summit shall our lives perforce be flung.
In the great world's battle-ages, even the cowards are
brave;
The winds of God are blowing, and we—ah, we are
young!

A Pilgrim Song.

AH, little Inn of Sorrow,
What of thy bitter bread?
What of thy ghostly chambers,
So I be shelterèd?
'Tis but for a night, the firelight
That gasps on thy cold hearthstone;
Tomorrow my load and the open road
And the far light leading on!

Ah, little Inn of Fortune,
What of thy blazing cheer,
Where glad through the pensive evening
Thy bright doors beckon clear?
Sweet sleep on thy balsam pillows,
Sweet wine that will assuage,
But send me forth o'er the morning earth
Strong for my pilgrimage!

Ah, distant End of the Journey,
What if thou fly my feet?
What if thou fade before me
In splendor wan and sweet?
Still the mystical city lureth—
The quest is the good knight's part;
And the pilgrim wends through the end of the ends
Toward a shrine and a Grail in his heart.

The Spring Moon.

DELICATE, scintillant Crescent-Lady,
What do you seek through the fields of blue?
Daintily going through April-blowing,
O young Moon-Lady, may I go too?

Adream you walk in your soft blue meadows,
With a chance-plucked flower in your spun-gold hair,
And a cloud-scarf trailing of silver veiling
And a Star-Child stumbling beside you there!

Bluet, and larkspur, and violet purple—
Knee-deep in the azure the Star-Child goes:
And where you are leading her all unheeding
O light Moon-Lady, who knows, who knows?

But oh, I wish that my feet were scaling
Your floating ladder let down for me!
For who would reckon when faeries beckon
And the witch-moon shines through the willow-tree?

The Votary.

"AND what is my wage for serving thee,
Heavenly lady, Poesy?"

"Blind through the sand-storm thou must ride
For a cactus-bloom in the desert wide.
Satin and flame, it shall light the way,
And thou wilt ride for it, come what may!"

"But what shall stand of the tower I've wrought,
With mortar of passion and stones of thought?"

"A grass-grown cairn where a stripling lone
Shall touch his lips to a crumbling stone,
And bow himself in the whispering dust.
But thou wilt build it—for build thou must!"

"And hast thou then no gifts for me,
Heavenly niggard, Poesy?"

"Yea, I will be to thee wheaten bread,
Purple and damask and swan's-down bed.
I let thee look on my face and live,
O mortal lover! Why should I give?"

The Lighthouse.

THE shadow of the lighthouse falls
Beside my window in the day;
By night a sturdy friend is he—
The tall, dim lantern by the bay.

Yet I, his neighbor, only see
A dusky tower, a hooded light;
He hoards his strength and flings it far
To guide the vessels through the night.

My Poet, too, is often dark
To idle gazers near at hand;
He may not shed his garnered light
On easy folk that hug the land;

But they that quest across the deep,
That roam, and cannot choose but roam,—
To them he sends a gallant beam
Across the thunder and the foam!

Birds in the City.

WHEN, after daisied lane and village street,
I found again the throbbing thoroughfare,
And, tingling to the rhythm of hurrying feet,
Yet missed a grace, a beauty from the air,

I scarce could name it; till today, chance-led
A little from the cheerful hum apart,
I entered this green domain of the dead
And stood within the city's sleeping heart.

And lo, the airy commerce I had missed!
The stir, the flutter in the busy air!
While, under the song-bubbles, still persist
The mockingbird's wild fountains, everywhere!

The cuckoo chuckles, willow-screened, above
A granite cross; and where its shadow falls
There passes, in an eddying flash of love,
The scarlet wooing of the cardinals.

Behold; they fill with mirth the silent place!
Back there, where men make merry and are gay,
I missed their delicate delight; here grace
Flutters above still sorrows laid away.

And thou, above thy meek, grey friar's coat,
Thou Bacchus-hearted, drunken with the spring,
Emptying still thy soft and thrilling throat,
Untouched by all my wonder, thou dost sing.

Poised high on drapèd urn, or broken bow,
Or hand that points to some conjectured sky,
Above the smitten hopes of men laid low
Still palpitates thy pagan ecstasy!

Quite careless of my chiding, thou wilt weave
Thy soft-lined home above the fallen head,
And keep, at night, where chilly angels grieve,
Thy rapture-haunted sleep above the dead.

Nodding in singing-robes thou wilt not doff,
Thou'lt wake to memory, with thy lyric loud,
Some burning heart, that has with pain put off
The poisoned shirt of passion for his shroud—

Who knows? or fright some little ghost, once well
Beloved, that now goes whimpering all the night,
And creeps again into its breathless cell,
Just as thy hungry ones acclaim the light.

Did He who snuffed flame after struggling flame
Send thee to flaunt thy primal raptures here?
See to what dim estate man's splendor came!
Why should He hold thy small perfection dear?

Ah, little brother! Vainly I protest!
Let Him appraise thy passion and my prayer
Who draws the daisies from this dead man's breast
And lends me Beauty to blindfold Despair!

The Moor-child.

AND you tempt me into your House of Love—
I, who have come from far
Through wintry forest and homeless heath,
Friend of the wind and star?
Ah, I fear me the warmth of the ingleside
And the depths of your dear caress
Will make me forget what I learned out there
In the stubble and loneliness!

Ah, the sheltered folk in the House of Love,
I have watched them, how blind they grow!
They cannot feel for the folk outside
Who walk barefoot in the snow.
For love is a mantle and love is a fire
And love is a velvet dress;
I have seen them pass as I roamed the moor
In my rags and nakedness.

I have long made friends with the open sky—
Rough are its ways, but true;
It will smile or frown on our cottage roof
After I come to you.
Oh, running I come to your house, good man,
But let us not close the door!
Leave a crack for the wail of the homeless wind
And the scudding rain of the moor!

Rondel for September.

YOU thought it was a falling leaf we heard:
I knew it was the Summer's gypsy feet;
A sound so reticent it scarcely stirred
The ear so still a message to repeat,—
"I go, and lo, I make my going sweet."
What wonder you should miss so soft a word?
You thought it was a falling leaf we heard:
I knew it was the Summer's gypsy feet.

With slender torches for her service meet
The golden-rod is coming; softer slurred
Midsummer noises take a note replete
With hint of change; who told the mocking-bird?
I knew it was the Summer's gypsy feet—
You thought it was a falling leaf we heard.

Heart's October.

AND shall I clutch at dear departing things
While leaf and tree in silent splendor part?
Go, little joys! and welcome, fluttering wings
That brush my clinging sorrows from my heart!

God's Prisoner.

LORD of wide spaces, though I wear Thy chains,
Duty, and circumstance, and body's pains,
Help thou my soul to mock Thy prison-bars,
And range Thy purple paths between the stars!

Wisdom.

LINE upon line, a little here and there,
We scrape together wisdom with slow care.
Wherefore? To blossom in a churchyard rose,
Or to go with the spirit—if it goes?

After Writing "Occasional Verses."

THE stars, my comrades, stand aloof from me:
They say I wrought today with smiles for hire.
The firefly winking past the maple-tree
He shames me with his small, essential fire.

W. V. M.

(1910)

DEAD—even he. They told me, and that day
Somehow my dreams went wailing, lost in space,
Finding the beggared earth a homeless place.
Then, as Death's violence to that vital clay
Slipped from my heart (as, Heaven be thanked, it may),
I saw his passing had but served to trace
A subtler line in life's mysterious face:
He is more friendly since he went away.

Grief is the treasure of his own: but I
Who only touched his garment's hem, draw near
And find in him increasingly my part,
Fall into step, bespeak his company!
Living, the nearest claim them; but the dear
Great dead belong to any humble heart.

The Young Envoy.

THEY sent me, but I must have lost my way—
The Voices yonder—and they bade me come,
Else I had fain stayed with the rest at home;
And they said "Speak!" but try as still I may
I have forgotten what they bade me say.
Ah, but 'twas noble! By it, eloquent Rome
Seemed but a noise of tumult; and mere foam
Of sunny seas was Athens' little day.

What was the word They gave me? Now and then
The thrushes start to sing it, and the breeze
Loitering by my ear when spring's at hand
Says a soft word in passing; then again
Goes murmuring off, high up among the trees,
Is gone, and I—I did not understand!

Bluebird and Cardinal.

I

THOU wingèd symbol of the quiet mind,
Thou straying violet, flying flower of spring,
Heaven-hued and heaven-hearted! Thou dost sing
As thou some sweet remembered thought didst find,
And, counselling with thyself in musing kind,
Didst softly say it over. Thy swift wing
Knows but a quiet rhythm; thou a thing
Of peace, to passion innocently blind.

Thy russet breast means married love, long hope,
Sheltered experience, small and sweet and sure,
All of the brown earth's natural purity;
But something heavenly, beyond our scope,
Steeped thy blue wing in color strange and pure,
Intense and holy as the mirrored sky.

II

Pulse of the gorgeous world, jubilant, strong,—
Thy song a whistled splendor, and thy coat
A fiery song! From thy triumphant throat
How I have heard it pouring, loud and long,
Whipping the air as with a scarlet thong—
The joyous lashing of thy triple note
Which all the tamer noonday noises smote
And clove a royal pathway through the throng!

Thou singest joy of battle, joy of fame,
Glory, and love of woman; joy of strife

With life's wild fates; and scorn'st, with jocund breath
For prudence' sake to dim thy feathered flame—
Thou heart of fire, epitome of life,
Full-throated flouter of vindictive death!

III

And lo, among the leafy, hidden groves
Within my heart, they both do flit and nest,
Saintly blue wing and vaunting scarlet crest,
Yea, all of life and all its myriad loves.
Even as Nature holds them, sifts and proves
And balances, so shall my soul find rest
In Her large tolerance, which without rest
Or lagging, toward some wide conclusion moves.

So, though I weary sometimes of the stress,
Leave me not, little lovers of the air,
Dearest of Nature's fine antithises!
Thou of the musing voice and heavenly dress,
Thou, royal firebrand,—neither could I spare,
My scarlet Passion, nor my wingèd Peace!

Brother-singers.

(1905)

I

BRAVE voices of the latter days, sing on!
Heed not the querulous and scornful cry
That bids you sing as in the days gone by
Sang the great lordly masters that are gone,
Else, leaving your meek service all undone,
Prostrate upon the temple-steps, to die.
That were an offering too cowardly:
Better a withered laurel, hardly won.

O Brother-singers! patient, eager—well
Ye know no man may name the day and hour!
Twilight of eve or morning, who can tell?
Soft, meek, the late birds in the dewy bower
Chirp after sunset; ay, and softer still
Ere first they greet the Sun upon the hill!

II

Yea, and the golden ages old men praise—
And young men, weak with noble youth's distress—
Were but the same wight in another dress:
Those wondrous days were even as these days:
Wonder walks muffled by familiar ways.
Much baseness, some far-shining nobleness,
Much striving, and a little high success,
Much singing, and a few immortal bays.

But ye, whom love hath chastened, who are ye
To stand dismayed before the waste of life?

Ye know of old to strive, and not to flee:
Victory's a guest, but an old friend is strife;
And Beauty, who forgets no child of hers,
Is tender toward her nameless ministers.

III

The Lords of Song went out to meet their fate
As we, high-hearted, but beset by pain,
Doubt, fear,—even as the youngest who would gain
The height, in these our days that seem so late.
Not for them all did fortune smile and wait:
Envying another's scope, years spent in vain
Seemed many years to Shakespeare; light disdain
And evil tongues passed the blind Milton's gate.

Ah, brothers! there is sea, and sky, and air,
And human hearts and faces; there is flame
Still in these living censers that we bear
Warm in our bosoms; heed not timid blame!
Stand close, and sing! Which one, by God's good grace,
Shall catch the morning on his upturned face?

To the Evening Star.

SILENT and sudden from the afterglow
Thou comest, O thou light of heaven's eyes!
Thou little sister of the soul, so wise
And innocent, with thy white looks aglow!
So smiles a certain little maid I know,
Returning, with that steadfast unsurprise
The yearning tendernesses that arise
In world-worn eyes that watch her beauty grow.

O virgin bride of splendor! soul of night!
Long before Wordsworth worshipped thee, or Keats
Sighed thee his swan-song, in thy censer white
Were stored old poets' dreams—the rarest sweets
Of earth—and thou dost pour them out for me
With all their starry looks at sight of thee!

The Dusty Way.

ALAS, these days of mine, how dim and low!
This mole-like soul, still digging through the dust
While up above the thin, obscuring crust
Of wont and usage, God's primroses grow,
And His great winds out of His spaces blow—
My life an aching sense of greatness lost.
A shiftless clerk, I take the days on trust,
Nor strip them of their spoil before they go.
Oh, rare-returning days of quickening strife,
And sentient calm, when the little minutes sing,
And the strong years take lovely hopes to wife,
And I can seem to see this round world swing
A shining apple on the Tree of Life
Set in the midst of God's fair gardening.

As Some Wrecked Sailor.

AS some wrecked sailor, cast up by the wave
Upon the green breast of some kindly land
Where no man dwells to share his sole command,
And he is Nature's guest, nor needs to crave
Her bounty, nor gird up his loins to brave
Dangers, but takes by stretching forth his hand;
Yet grows to hate the glittering yellow sand,
And finds his peace but stillness of the grave:—
Even such am I, who walk this sheltered vale
Of quiet joys kind hearts have made for me;
So feel I secret springs of being fail
To taste again the quickening agony:
The salty wind, and—throbbing through the gale,
Thundering under me once again—the Sea!

Veiled Moonlight.

THERE is no passion in the world tonight:
No waking bird's small liquid jet of song,
No dank wood-wind with faint enchantments strong,
No amorous moon to pour down throbbing light
On the desirous meadows; sickly-bright
She threads her way the listless clouds among;
And none can say the world was ever young,
And none can prove the dream of youth was right!
O thou, my lost illusion! O thou Doubt,
With subtle eyes and pale, destroying hands!
Thou walkest with me, hedging me about
With sad philosophies from wise old lands,—
And all my passionate days are spent, poured out
Like rich wine spilt upon the desert sands!

"The Heart Knoweth—"

SOMETIMES my little woe is lulled to rest,
Its clamor shamed by some old poet's page—
Tumult of hurrying hoof, and battle-rage,
And dying knight, and trampled warrior-crest.
Stern faces, old heroic souls unblest,
Eye me with scorn, as they my grief would gauge
A mere child, schooled to weep upon the stage,
Tricked for a part of woe, and sombre-drest.
"Lo, who art thou," they ask, "that thou shouldst fret
To find, forsooth, one single heart undone?
The page thou turnest there is purple-wet
With blood that gushed from Cæsar overthrown!
Lo, who art thou to prate of sorrow?" Yet
This little woe, it is my own, my own!

"Two Loves I Have—"

"TWO loves I have of comfort and despair":
One, that divine up-groping toward the sun
That men call Art; and one—ah heart!—and one
The mortal pain the gods came down to wear.
And Art and Love are lovers; she is fair
And fleet, and coy—when Love is gay—to run
Beyond his reach, and leave to him alone
The mocking light of her back-streaming hair.
But when Love bows in heaviness, the tear
Of old despairs upon his proud cheek wet,
He hears her whispering sandals drawing near;
And pausing, stung by passionate regret,
She sings for pity, careless who may hear,
If haply he may listen and forget.

The Old Inn.

THE air is keen; Yule-tide is at the door;
  And like an old inn is this heart of mine,
Where once beneath the holly and the pine
Mine host himself brought in the bay-decked boar;
And, while the Yule-log made the rafters roar,
Old beaux and wits made merry o'er their wine.
Its glory is departed; 'neath its sign
The gayer guests regale themselves no more.
Mine host, long since grown tottering and grey,
Makes feeble cheer about the chimney vast;
Bids wine and feasting in the good old way,
Welcomes his humbler guests to their repast;
Then sits unheeding mid the mirth and games
And watches the old faces in the flames.

"Desire of Fame."

SEE, how I wrestle with the stubborn days,
Morn, noon and eve, and will not let them go
Except they bless me. In the steps of slow
Reticent Time I follow; subtle ways
Of Art and Knowledge spread their baffling maze
Before my feet; but doughty blow on blow
I fight the high, hard battle, and will know
No truce, till on my forehead rest the bays.

Yet, sometimes in the struggle, when the thirst
Of effort tortures, and the thwarted will
Devours the heart, 'tis deeper pain, that this
Is that same soul I used to be, when first,
O early love! thou couldst so surely fill
These dusty wells to brimming, with—a kiss!

Evening.

GO, little sorrows! From the evening wood
Faint odors rise, that touch the heart like tears
With inarticulate comfort. Lo, she bears
A weary load—small cares that drug the blood,
Small envies, sick desires for lesser good—
All day, till now the evening reappears,
They drop away, and she with wonder rears
Her aching height from needless servitude.
The tree-tops are all music; light and soft
The brook's small feet go tinkling toward the sea
Bearing the little day's distress afar;
While yonder, in the stillness set aloft,
My one great Grief, still glimmering down on me,
Smiles tremulous as a bereavèd Star.

To My Masters.

BENEATH this dower of unquiet heart
And lonely spirit not for long appeased,
Sometimes I murmur, "Would that it had pleased
The gods to mete to me a simpler part,
A common compass and a plainer chart;
The acquiescence whereby men are eased
Of the eternal question—of the teased
Sense of lost meanings, drowned in street and mart."

Then ye arise before me; and ye wear
Even in your eyes your spirits' many scars.
O piteous lords of sorrow! I forswear
The peace I late lamented; for these wars
Gird on my sword! Enough that I shall share
The dear, brief smile of your unhappy stars.

The Tyrant.

I MADE a covenant with Time. He spake:
"O braggart brain, presumptuous heart of dust,
Brief energy, dost fret at moth and rust?
Think'st thou to mend the laggard pace I take?
Behold the hills—the baubles that I make—
Bow down before me: verily thou must!
Then grudge not, stint not, brave the world's distrust,
Wait and stand steadfast while I make and break:—

Then see how generous old Time can be!
Then rest, and be his darling! Ho, the sheaves
These hasty folk snatch from my granary,
Then, startled at my shadow, drop like thieves!
I chuckle as I lay them by for thee,
Mellow as sunlight in autumnal eves!"

The Young Poet to Italy.

O BEAUTIFUL, O dear beyond desire,
Sometimes fond fears assail me, when the day
Is long, and Fame and Fortune still delay,
Lest thou, who waitest for me there, should'st tire,
Saying, "He hath forgotten his old sire,
Hoary Antiquity—his pensive, gay,
And tender mother, Beauty; he will stay,
Poor changeling! by the alien household fire."

Then I remember all the storied years
That thou wert thou, before my life began;
Take courage, and laugh softly at my fears:
What matter though I linger half my span?
Thou wilt not fade, nor sink into the sea,
A few more years, till I can come to thee!

In a National Cemetery.

SLEEPING, still sleeping, after all the years!
My earliest memory recalls them so,
Stretching away, white row upon white row.
'Tis meet the sward still velvet green appears,
The wall its solemn weight of ivy wears;
But they, so many men with blood aglow!
To see them still so patiently laid low,
It stirs a pain too passionate for tears.

Strange! For the buried struggle had grown tame
When first my father told it me: the ires
Of battle but a story and a name;
Yet, still they sleep as one who never tires,
And still, where autumn sets the trees aflame,
Some ghostly sentinel tends their signal-fires.

The Site of an Old Mission.

(1690)

(The exact location of the first Spanish mission in Texas is not now known. Father Manzanet, its founder, says that the chief of the Tejas allowed him to select it, and that he chose "a delightful spot close by a brook, with fine woods, and plum-trees like those in Spain.")

NO cross is left to mark it; yet to me
It seems that I should know it! I should know
The brook that pleased the holy father so,
The flowering plums that sent his memory
Back to his lovely Spain beyond the sea—
When, on that kind May morning long ago,
Surveying all the simple chief could show,
He marked the spot for that lone sacristy.

O flower of faith sown in the wilderness!
Thy visible petals are but dust again,
And where they fell we may but seek and guess;
Yet there must linger still the chant's refrain,
And incense mingle, at the wind's caress,
With breath of plum-trees "like the ones in Spain"!

A Remembered Parable.

MY Castle of Delight upon the sand
I builded; yellow sands beside a sea
Where the mermaidens' singing eerily
Haunted the turrets—an enchanted land,
Reborn at every wandering wind's command!
Foredoomed it was a bitter day should be
That swept my towered dream away from me,
My many-chambered mansion love had planned!

Now, after homeless years, upon the rock
Of thee, I build my later House-of-Dreams;
And in thy keeping, safe from thunder-shock,
(Tho' light as mist above the magic streams)
My miracle, my fortress on the height,
It soars, with oriel windows burning bright!

To My Enemy.

UNDER thy yoke of spears, O Time, I go:
I, too, am mortal, though but yesterday
I lifted thy huge gauntlet where it lay
And flung it back with laughter. Now I know
Too well its grievous weight; it hath laid low
Youth's certitude at last. Man's crumbling clay
I took to be the gods' rock-paven way:
Hope lent the wingèd shoes; tired feet are slow.

I bow my neck; my soul I will not bow.
Though now I may not bear my torch so high
As when, its gusty light upon my brow,
I danced derision of thy tyranny;
Still, 'tis a torch I bear—a brand that thou
Must seize, fling down, yea, trample, ere it die!

After Youth.

I

AND gazest thou in Beauty's eyes
All shriven of desire,
Content with humblest ministries
That feed her sacred fire?

Look'st thou on youth thou would'st not tame
As some high tourney-field,
Some ardent, wind-imperilled flame
Thy brooding hand would shield?

Friend, thou may'st still defy thy cares,
Still find a balm for ruth,—
But gone, ah, gone the haunted airs
That blew across thy youth!

II

Youth's house was empty:
Love entered in.
Then there was feasting
Where fast had been!

Life's house was empty:
Poor Love was dead.
Through another portal
Grief came, instead.

Love's house was empty,
Grief, gone her way.
Sweet Maiden Memory
Came there to stay.

III

Ah me, the April air was sweet,
The white clouds floated high,
When we fared forth with laughing feet,
My lover, Life, and I!

Then, lackaday! The evil case
When lovers sundered be!
In grief I fled the cruel face
Of Life, mine enemy.

Now we sit resting on the stile,
Quiet as man and wife.
Sure, I shall trudge yet many a mile
With my old crony, Life!

Poet Songs.

I

I SHALL not get my poem done
Or hardly started, even;
But God will understand, I think,
And let me work in Heaven.

Or, if His plan is different
For Love, and Toil, and Art,
He'll let some red, appeasing flower
Burst from my buried heart.

II

I cast my nets in many streams
To catch the silver fish of dreams:
In vain I pant, pursue and dip—
They through the straining meshes slip.

And still I go my bootless ways
Through starry nights and striving days,
With naught to show for all my greed
But bits of shell and water-weed.

III

Dropp'd feathers from the wings of God
My little songs and snatches are,
So light He does not hear them fall
As He goes by, from star to star.

Dropp'd feathers from the wings of God
I find, and braid them in my hair;
Men heed them not—they only make
My soul unto herself more fair.

A Child's Game.

NOR sleep, nor journey, nor affray
Can justly image death to me:
I am a little child, and Death
The one who lets you go and see.

All children in a darkened room;
And Death stands smiling at the door,
His finger on his lips, and says
So quietly, "Now, one child more!"

I have so longed and longed to know
What lovely things the children find
When they have gone beyond the door;
But not a child that's left behind

Has ever been; for when they go
He will not ever let them back:
And when he beckons them, and we
Stand tiptoe, watching for the crack,

Our strange, sweet playmate steps between
And will not let us see at all;
He smiles at our expectancy
With "You may come, too, when I call."

And oh, within the darkened room,
I have so longed and longed to know
Just what it is they see and learn,
The other children, when they go.

Do you suppose that I shall feel
Afraid, to see him look at me,
At last, and beckon with his hand,
And smile, "Now *you* may go and see"?

Bed-time.

SHALL I yield up this shallow breath
For breathings full and deep,
Some night into the hands of Death,
As now, tonight, to Sleep?

Shall I not know that peace is best,
As I am sure tonight,
Nor grudge a tired heart its rest
From sorrow and delight?

So gladly come, as one who brings
His soul for God to keep,
To be washed clean among the springs
Of silence and of sleep?

Yea, and betake me to my urn
As to my bed tonight—
A place to tarry and unlearn
Until the morning light.

Flower of Life.

THEY say my living soul must scale
The beetling crags of death,
Still, on those glittering ramparts, breathe
With memory's laboring breath,

Else, it were waste incredible—
Life's long, up-groping pain;
Its glory born of dust, to go
Into the dust again.

But ah, where is that early love
More mine than hand or eye?
What splendor may not fade and pass
If youth and love may die?

Where is their heaven for my dog?
Where is that finer part—
Irrelevant unto the dust
That wraps his faithful heart?

What profit hath the daffodil
Of her ethereal flame?
It flickers down the wind, to join
The fires whence it came.

And I—what if this æon-bought,
Wind-beaten soul of mine
Were but the highest flower of all
On Life's up-clambering vine?

The petals fall, the perfume spills
Upon the timeless hours:
The great trunk toiling up the cliff
Climbs on—but thinks in flowers!

Creeds.

FRIEND, you are grieved that I should go
Unhoused, unsheltered, gaunt and free,
My cloak for armor—for my tent
The roadside tree;

And I—I know not how you bear
A roof betwixt you and the blue.
Brother, the creed would stifle me
That shelters you.

Yet, that same light that floods at dawn
Your cloistered room, your cryptic stair,
Wakes me, too—sleeping by the hedge—
To morning prayer!

The Dead Forerunner.

DO you hear the women marching, little mother,
Where you slumber in your narrow bed apart,
With your little hands locked fast,
Icy, motionless, at last,
Above the ashen crater of your heart?
You, the passionate forerunner of the morrow,
You, who died before the breaking of the light,
Frail, Promethean foe of hoary wrong and sorrow,
Can you hear the women marching through the night?

Not so piteous the lot of those who perished
Long years before the breaking of the day,
Who took into their graves the vision cherished
With fruition still milleniums away!
But the army you awaited, Banner-Bearer,
Was just around the corner of the years!
O little dauntless ghost,
Was it you who led the host
When I watched it flashing past me, through my tears?

Can you hear the women marching, little mother,
In the narrow little bed where you sleep?
All the crowding, hurrying feet,
Marching with victorious beat
Above the graves of sowers—these who reap?
O, I think my heart could bear its mem'ries better,
Recall, without so passionate a tear,
Your soul's unconquered wearing of the fetter,
If only you could know the day is here!

They are coming, they are coming, little mother,
Some with fierce, fanatic sword and foolish spear,
But the many girt with love of son and brother,
Mother-tolerance, and sturdy mother-cheer.
But I wish that you could see them, thronging, singing,
Up the lonely path the lantern-bearers trod,
On the journey of the soul
Toward the ever-luring goal
Of man, the tireless traveller to God!

To the Marching Women.

MAY I, then, salute the banner, where it streams above the throngs,
I, who linger by the hedgerows, making up my soldier-songs?
See, I wear no plume of courage, bear no sword of saint or seer—
May I pipe a little marching-tune 'twill hearten you to hear?

O ye sturdy, marching women, with your tolerance and scorn,
My mother would have fared with you, and I of her am born;
I love you and I thrill to you—but, pray you let me stay
A Keeper of the Vision on the hills above the fray!

Here beside the ancient hearthstone I am friend to bond and free,
For my soul is on the headland, looking, laughing, out to sea!
For no boon of tool or weapon is the vow of thanks I make:
In the salty wind of freedom is the gift of God I take!

O Sisters, let me sing to you, who trudge the dusty way!
I will make the vision glow again, that needs must flicker grey!
From my peaceful hills of fancy I will send my fighting Song,
A stripling with a fiery sword to beckon you along!

Mother-song.

WITHIN Life's throne-room, hushed and dim,
Spent I shall lie, and still,
Whilst thou thy small, indignant breast,
O little soul, shalt fill
With breath of strange mortality
And send thy homeless cry
A-groping for thy mother's heart,
Where, spent and still, I lie.

Oh, if God, entering there, should leave
That august door ajar,
And let the Wind that stirs His robe
Chill-blowing from afar,
Puff out my spirit like a flame
That dieth in the night—
God shield *thee* with His hollowed hand,
O little, little Light!

Possessions.

ALL day he goes about his quest,
No connoisseur so keen as he:—
A spool, a bug, a piece of string,
A shoe-horn, thing of mystery,

A button or a domino,
All wrought of wonder and delight!
And when at last he seeks my arms
He holds his latest treasure tight,—

From eager habit clutching still
Some relic of his miser's store;
Until, his busy day forgot,
He lets it clatter to the floor.

And I, who hold him to my breast,
Pearl of my crowded treasury,—
(Ah me, the hunger of the world
Hath bitten wiser folk than he!)

I, too,—they say,—from Her deep arms
(That last great mother of us all)
Shall drop my dearly-hoarded joys
Nor stir, nor miss them when they fall!

Reprieve.

THE other day it dawned on me,
A sudden shock across our play:
He is so old—the miracle
May happen any day!

The miracle: at any hour
This small man-comrade at my knee
May take upon his soul his first
Clear memory of me.

Some trivial moment, slackened mood
Imperishably there may trace
My picture, as at heart I bear
My sweet dead mother's face.

I—I, unworthy. Let me bow
(Like kneeling page of old, to feel
Laid on my shoulder, stiff and shrewd,
The consecrating steel)

Abased in utter thankfulness
Before the mirror of his eyes:
He is so little yet—I still
May make his memories!

The Housemother.

THEY cling to the skirts of my spirit with their tiny,
implacable clutch;
With the bonds of my love they enmesh me, woven close
by their satin-soft touch;
Not an hour of their clamorous waking they spare me,
the whole day through,
Till the weight on my wings is an anguish, and I faint
for the fetterless blue.
Then—washed by the wild wind of freedom that sweeps
from the heavenly steep,
I swoop from the violet spaces to hover and bless them,
asleep!

I bring him his wheat-bread and honey, I run for his
sandals and staff;
Though the day may have drained me, at evening I must
still be his goblet to quaff.
Dear despot of love, little recks he of vigils untamed that
I keep,
I, the server, who rise from my pillow, to watch him, ful-
filled and asleep.
Then I toss back the hair of my spirit, bare my feet for
the heavenly streams,
And range with him, lover and lover, hand in hand
through the world of his dreams!

Apple and Rose.

MY little daughter is a tea-rose,
Satin to the touch,
Wine to the lips,
And a faint, delirious perfume.

But my little son
Is a June apple,
Firm and cool,
And scornful of too much sweetness,
But full of tang and flavor
And better than bread to the hungry.

O wild winds and clumsy, pilfering bees,
With the whole world to be wanton in,
Will you not spare my little tea-rose?
And O ruthless blind creatures,
Who lay eggs of evil at the core of life,
Pass by my one red apple,
That is so firm and sound!

A Little Boy's Bath.

YOU would have thought he never would come clean,
Yet here he is, shining like a sea-shell.

O Life, thou secret-hearted, ancient mother,
Teach him the hidden paths to thy rock-fountains,
Make them plain to his feet,
And for the insult of thy deep pollutions,
The dust, and sweaty grime, and clinging foulness,
Give him to know thy laughing water-courses,
And the clean brown pools
Among the rocks.

I, his mother, have jealously kept his firm, small body:
Keep thou his soul, O Life!

Stillness.

AS a gull loves the sea-spray,
So I love stillness.
I love to creep
Under a blanket of stillness that muffles even the beat of my heart,
And tuck it in under my chin—or draw it up over my head.
I do not always want the feet of other people
Muddying up the springs of my mind.
Even the feet of the children, as they come whooping and splashing,
Shatter, unknowing, the fragile, bright mirror,
Often,
And send the leaves of my sky-trees flying in every direction,
And drown the strange flowers.
But then—the little feet themselves are so sweet!

Beach-play.

WE count the waves, O little son—
You whom with pain I bore:
And you will be the sea, I know,
And I must be the shore.

O youth, the unappeasable
That can but break, and break!
I think I shall be very wise
For youth's remembered sake.

Summer Song.

OH, you are lovely, my lady South,
With weariest eyes and rose-sweet mouth,
As I sit and fan you and braid up your hair;
But if I were a man, do you think I'd stay
With a clinging, mistress-love alway,
And the chains that you make men wear?

Oh, I'd hie me out of your white-walled house
And I'd cut me a bed of balsam-boughs,
Where the cloud-sails tug at the lodge-pole spars;
And over the crest of the Great Divide
I'd woo me the West for a free man's bride,
And I'd climb with her—to the stars!

For the Rockies.

THERE are two big cottonwoods
In the yard of my neighbor down the street.
And often,
When I pass there,
On a dusty morning in midsummer
When the air has dropped dead,
I see the alfalfa growing under the red mesas
And the gold hay-stacks in the high hay-fields.
And my soul pants for the snow-fed waters,
And my body hungers for the mountain-manna,
And my heart is sick with a great longing
For a strange land.

Faery Mountains.

ALL summer long, sick for the mountains,
Crouched under the scourge of the heat,
I found them one night, of a sudden,
At the end of my own village street!

Sheer, shadowy cliffs cutting skyward:
Wooded slopes, soaring daintily!
(By day 'twas our little church-steeple
And a neighborly sycamore-tree—

But Beauty had found them, and set them,
Her heavenly avatars,
With a little blue valley between them
Prickling all over with stars.)

So now, when the long day is ended,
And the sun his last javelin has hurled,
My heart climbs the sycamore mountains
And drinks all the winds of the world!

Some Fellow-poets.

I LOVE to see them sitting solemnly,
Holding their souls like watches to their ears,
And shouting, every time they tick, "A Poem!"

Keats and Fanny Brawne.

HE tried to pour the torrents of his love
Into a tiny vase; a trinket—smooth,
Pretty enough—but fit to hold a rose
Upon some shrewd collector's cabinet.
Toward this small moon the wild tides of his love
Reared up, and fell back, moaning; and he died
Asking himself why love was agony.

And she? She loved the best she could, I think,
And wondered sometimes—but not overmuch—
At poor John's queer, unseemly violence.

The Family.

IN church I watched the preacher's wife and son,
A kind, broad-bosomed woman, and a boy
Still in knee-trousers, but already well
Above his mother's shoulder. He would please her—
One saw that; none the less, his sulky thoughts
Rose up and settled on his Sunday face
Like smoke upon a glass. She let him lean
His great head on her cushioned arm, and yawn,
And watch his father while he preached and preached
With solemn words all tangled in his beard.
But when, the benediction said, she turned,
He was not there; while still the blessing hung
In air, he'd bolted. She looked after him
And smiled. . . . She did not know I saw her smile.

At the Picture-show.

SHE sits with eyes intent upon the screen,
A quiet woman with work-hardened hands.
Beside her squirms an eager, shock-head boy;
Upon her lap a little rumpled girl
With petaled cheek and bright, play-roughened hair;
While, bulwark of the little family group,
Her husband looms, with one unconscious arm
Lying along her chair-back. So they come
Often, and for a few cents, more or less,
Slip through the wicket-gate of wonderment
That bounds the beaten paths of everyday.
The Indians and the horses thrill the boy
With dreams of great adventure; the big man
Likes the great bridges, and the curious lore
Of alien folk in other lands; the child
Laughs at the funny way the people die.
And she?

The way the hero's overcoat
Sets to his shoulders; or a lock of hair
Tossed back impatiently; or else a smile,
A visible sigh, an eyebrow lifted, so,—
They touch strange, buried, dispossessed old dreams.
And while her hand plays with the baby's curls
Unthinking, once again she sees the face
That swayed her youth as ocean tides are swayed
Until she broke her heart to save her soul . . .
And fled back to her native town . . . and left
In the grey canyons of the city streets
All the high hopes of youth. . . .

She has picked up
Her life since then, and made a goodly thing
Out of the fragments; that is written plain
Upon the simple page for all to see.
I fancy that she hardly thinks of him
Through all her wholesome days; but when, at night,
They go a-voyaging across the screen,
And suddenly a street-lamp throws a gleam
On a wet pavement . . . a man sits alone
On a park bench . . . or else goes swinging past
With that expression to his overcoat . . .
She does not pick this player-man, or that,
But all the heroes have some trick of his. . . .

From the Pullman.

ALL day I have sat gazing out of the window,
Blessing my eyes with the silver of the little bare trees.
But now, in the dark,
I am haunted by the faces of women in lonely shanties—
Here an old one, there a young one, but always a woman
In the half-opened door,
Watching the world go by.

Unser Gott.

(1914)

THEY held a great prayer-service in Berlin,
And augured German triumph from some words
Said to be spoken by the Jewish God
To Gideon, which signified that He
Was staunchly partial to the Israelites.
The aisles were thronged; and in the royal box
(I had it from a tourist who was there,
Clutching her passport, anxious, like the rest,)
There sat the Kaiser, looking "very sad."
And then they sang; she said it shook the heart.
The women sobbed; tears salted bearded lips
Unheeded; and my friend looked back and saw
A young girl crumple in her mother's arms.
They carried out a score of them, she said,
While German hearts, through bursting German throats
Poured out, *Ein Feste Burg Ist Unser Gott!*

(Yea, "Unser Gott! Our strength is *Unser* Gott!
Not that light-minded Bon Dieu of France!")

I think we all have made our God too small.
There was a young man, a good while ago,
Who taught that doctrine . . . but they murdered him
Because he wished to share the Jewish God
With other folk.

They are long-lived, these fierce
Old hating gods of nations; but at last
There surely will be spilled enough of blood

To drown them all! The deeps of sea and air,
Of old the seat of gods, no more are safe
For mines and monoplanes. The Germans, now,
Can surely find and rout the God of France
With Zeppelins, or some slim mother's son
Of Paris, or of Tours, or Brittany,
Can drop a bomb into the *Feste Burg,*
And, having crushed the source of German strength,
Die happy in his blazing monoplane.

Sad jesting! If there be no God at all,
Save in the heart of man, why, even so—
Yea, all the more—since we must make our God,
Oh, let us make Him large enough for all,
Or cease to prate of Him! If kings must fight,
Let them fight for their glory, openly,
And plain men for their lands and for their homes,
And heady youths, who go to see the fun,
Blaspheme not God. True, maybe we might leave
The God of Germany to some poor frau
Who cannot go, who can but wait and mourn,
Except that she will teach him to her sons—
A God quite scornful of the Slavic soul,
And much concerned to keep Alsace-Lorraine.
They should go godless, too,—the poor, benumbed,
Crushed, anguished women, till their hearts can hold
A greater Comforter!

(Yet it is hard
To make Him big enough! For me, I like
The English and the Germans and the French,
The Russians, too; and Servians, I should think,
Might well be very interesting to God.

But do the best I may, my God is white,
And hardly takes a nigger seriously
This side of Africa. Not those, at least,
Who steal my wood, and of a summer night
Keep me awake with shouting, where they sit
With monkey-like fidelity and glee
Grinding through their well-oiled sausage-mill—,
The dead machinery of the white man's church—
Raw jungle-fervor, mixed with scraps sucked dry
Of Israel's old sublimities: not those.
And when they threaten us, the Higher Race,
Think you, which side is God's? Oh, let us pray
(Lest blood yet spurt to wash that black skin white,
As now it flows because a German hates
A Cossack, and an Austrian a Serb!)

What was it that he said so long ago,
The young man who outgrew the Jewish God—
"Not a sparrow falleth—?" Ah, God, God,
And there shall fall a million murdered men!

In a Walled Garden.

(1917)

I LIVE on under my great trees,
Rearing butterflies and children,
And watching for the Canterbury bells,
While half the world bleeds—
Curses and bleeds.
All I do about it
Is to sew a few passionate seams
And save a little wheat.
(They tell me that some Yankee college-boy, impudent and adorable,
Some fair-haired, strapping cub who made the team,
Then broke loose, at the first call, from Berkeley or Cornell,
May keep strong and fit on the wheat I help to save:
Strong and fit
To die.)

Yet, when the pain grows unbearable, I think,
"But is it not for this that wars are fought,
That men die for a loved country,
After all:
To keep a place where life has light and room,
Where somebody has time for the tiny, endless needs of little children,
And Canterbury bells?"

So one of my souls moves on in its appointed orbit,
Luminous and glad,

And the other sits in the ashes,
Brooding,
Inconsolable,
Ashamed.

Eagle Youth.

(1918)

THEY have taken his horse and plume,
  They have left him to plod, and fume
For a hero's scope and room!
They have curbed his fighting pride,
They have bade him burrow and hide
With a million, side by side:
Look—into the air he springs,
Fighting with wings!

He has found a way to be free
Of that dun immensity
That would swallow up such as he:
Who would burrow when he could fly?
He will climb up into the sky
And the world shall watch him die!
Only his peers may dare
Follow him there!

Graves in France.

THEIR fates shall be a song, a schoolboy's wonder
 For many a day—
O the red treasure we have buried yonder,
So far away!

O the poor, panting love that must go weeping
Through bloody foam,
To find the soldier in his glory sleeping,
So far from home!

France, we have loved thee! But beyond all measure
Our love shall be,
Since in thy bosom we have hid our treasure
Of agony.

Street-doves.

MY soul is a flock of doves
Swooping and scrambling for grains of corn in the street,
And I am their master,
Vainly calling from a high casement.
Greedy birds, soiling your white bosoms,
Why do you not come oftener home,
And be still in my breast?

Wild Geese.

WILD goose, O wild goose,
Up in the high, wild weather,
Tarry a moment, O brother!
Let us go on together!

Yonder, at anchor,
Fowls of your selfsame feather,
Three fat burghers are dozing,
Tied with a thong of leather,

Till they hear you, wild brother,
And leap, and tug at the tether!
And oh, but my dream goes calling
Off through the high, wild weather!

Song.

WHERE do the sea-birds sleep?
On the waves breaking?
Sprayed by the plumy deep
Sleeping and waking?

When will my thoughts give o'er
Circling and flying?
Must they go evermore
Skimming and crying?

The Tapping Bush.

THE bare bush close to my window
 Taps and scratches on the glass—
Taps and scratches. . . .

It was a maiden once, with the wild heart of a poet,
Who would not come into the house
And be tamed.

And some fret at the pane from the inside,
And some from without.

The Ploughman.

GOD will not let my field lie fallow.

The ploughshare is sharp, the feet of His oxen are heavy;
They hurt.
But I cannot stay God from His ploughing,
I, the lord of the field.
While I stand waiting,
His shoulders loom upon me from the mist,
He has gone past me down the furrow, shouting a song.

(I had said, it shall rest for a season.
The larks had built in the grass. . . .)

He will not let my field lie fallow.

On the Highway.

A HARP among the willows,
My heart was young,
Wearying, complaining,
Lest Life, wild Life, the glorious mad harper,
Who tramped and shouted up and down the highway,
Forever should pass by it,
Hanging forever,
Aching and burning and sighing unfulfilled
For his crashing hand on the strings. . . .

Then of a sudden he snatched my harp in passing,
(My heart was young)
Smote it and slung it over his shoulder, laughing,
Pleased with its tingling newness. . . .

Lord, I am still thine instrument, I love thee,
As not so many love thee, I am faithful!
But oh, remember,
The strings grow thin, the harp has answered often—
Careful, O wild immortal troubadour!

In the City.

BACK at my home, where the village ends
And the furrowed land begins,
God is a music of cello-tones
And satiny violins.

But here, in this maelstrom of opposites,
This passion of splendors and slimes,
The factory chimneys are organ-pipes
And the engine-bells are chimes.

And which is dearer I cannot tell—
My blossomy symphony,
Or the thundering organ that breaks my heart
And sunders my soul from me.

Song.

MY soul is an Eagle
On the wind she rides.
But my heart is tender,
A nest-defender
(My heart is a Dove.)

My soul is scornful,
Nowhere she bides.
But my heart goes grieving
From too-long leaving
(I will turn home, Love.)

Smoke.

I AM the pearl of the earth,
The soul of the grime,
I am the delicate, visible mirth
Of the sorrow and slime.

I am the light in the sinner,
The wings in the clod,
I am the beautiful breath of The Brute
Praising God.

Breinigsville, PA USA
30 July 2010
242783BV00002B/19/A

9 781104 041380